INKLINGS
COMPLICITY

twenty poems

Michael
Bartholomew–Biggs

Pikestaff Press
2003

Published in 2003
by
Pikestaff Press
Ellon House : Harpford : Sidmouth : Devon EX10 0NH
Tel. (01395) 568941

Printed by Riverside Printing Services
Harpford

Copyright (c) Michael Bartholomew-Biggs 2003

ISBN 1 900974 23 1

British Library Cataloguing in Publication Data.
A catalogue record for this book is available from
the British Library.

ACKNOWLEDGEMENTS

Several of these poems have appeared before in one or other of the following: *Critical Survey; First Time; Iota; Other Poetry; Seam; Smiths Knoll; Spokes; Staple.* Grateful acknowledgement is due to the editors of these periodicals.

CONTENTS

Criminal Tendencies / 5
Moving Violation / 6
Bredon Hill / 7
Core Curriculum / 8
RE / 9
Don't Try This At Home / 10
Grand Mal / 11
For MJB Wherever This May Find Him / 12
Snapshot / 13
Pillar Box / 14
Warning Off / 15
Finding The Way / 16
Dungeness / 17
In Granada / 18
Nothing Outward / 19
Conversation Piece / 20
Sharp Practice / 21
The Whispering Knights / 22
Glastonbury Tor / 23
To Whom It May Concern / 24

For Nancy
with love

CRIMINAL TENDENCIES

I was talking in my sleep to this policeman.
What it is, he said, is this. You trust your judgement.
You get real close in up against your suspect
then you lean on him
(and here he rubbed his face on mine)
and you notice his reaction.
You can always tell the guilty ones.
Does it stand up well in court? He didn't answer
but applied his cheek again and I could feel
reactions that were asking to be noticed.
So I made an effort.
What I want to know, I said,
is how many of the people
get to pass your test and walk away?
None of them, he smiled, and that's the point.
That's the way we know we've got it right.

MOVING VIOLATION

Blame it on the shellfish is a simple rule:
maybe bouillabaisse
can imitate an enema?
D & V's a delicate abbreviation
but, taken short in Arles, it was precious little use
to observe I wasn't vomiting.

Often one's unsure what bitter fungus spoiled
a well-intentioned stew.
This time I knew which pinch of mischief
I'd had slipped to me in St Remy that morning:
while I'd picnicked, unsuspectingly, brisk thieves
had vandalised my car.

The gendarme chose to call the damage *degradation*,
which is what it felt like
as I took in the incident.
Those types who broke the lock undid my intestines,
which testified against them, with a steady stream
of — so to speak — invective.

BREDON HILL

We're out to let me wander in the past.
I came here camping as a child, believing
it adventurous to try my luck
at roughing it. On cold uncomfy nights
I shivered as I thought I caught the chill
of ragged ghosts who'd trudged this way to fight
at Tewkesbury and leave their smell to hang
alongside banners stale with spilled ambition.

Our reconstruction of the walk from Evesham,
in the car, seemed less an exploration
than I might have hoped. And now I'm here
I cannot recognize the site or find
the place in me so easily enchanted.
Not quite true. Whatever I pretend with
campfire quips, it's yet to be established
just how hard I really want to search,

being conscious that our company includes
a fourteen-year-old self in shorts. Embarrassed,
he's riding in the back with nothing much
to say – or nothing he has confidence
in offering as tentative improvement
on silence from the stranger who is driving
and doesn't care to stop and let him out
to saunter in the sunshine on his own.

CORE CURRICULUM

Frowning at the inkwell of learning
tongue thrust out through lips
labouring over letters
with a nib that splits
to spatter extra dots on all the i's
and cross the t's before we come to them.
Each character perfected
to help us form strong characters
we rehearse an alphabet
for spelling out our stories.

1950's child and this year's adult:
both striving for connections
to give our words the virtue of integrity
and – something that we learned about much later –
more value than their letters' algebraic sum.
There's still some doubt that either one will manage
to get to grips with proper joined-up writing.

RE

We had to make a time chart of the Bible.
I was eight and couldn't
draw straight lines to save my soul:
so Samson sprawled unkempt across the page
too close to Jezebel.
For weeks I dreaded punishment
would follow when I had to give it in;
but they never asked —
must have managed to forget
even if I can't.

What they did collect were diagrams
comparing synagogue
with parish church. My draughtsmanship
was little more adroit, the pews askew
as if the congregation
had run to catch the final trumpet.
This time they marked me with a final sentence:
"If you would only go
inside a church you'd find how much
of what you've done is wrong."

DON'T TRY THIS AT HOME

I could have been a footnote
in a lot of lives – the boy
they went to school with who
killed himself when he was twelve
and told nobody why.

Prowling through the house
my boredom saw the kitchen towel
looped around its roller on the door
and impulse simply slipped my head through
to let the time hang heavy
on my jugular and wind-pipe.

A helicopter squatted
in my skull with swishing rotors;
then private stars and pleasant pins-and-needles
accompanied my coming back
to atmospheric and hydraulic normal.

I tried that buzz again,
pushing dizziness a little harder.
Then harder still. I next remember
cool red tiles beneath my cheek
and my limbs spread artlessly
ready for the chalk-line.

Like angel wings above me
drooped two frayed ends of shabby fabric
my mother's slim defence
against the grime that touched my being
and botched attempts to wash my hands of both.

GRAND MAL

Misprints make him restless still
by being not quite wrong. Is this
another tiny crease preceding
total folding of the world
as images from either side
fail to match but dip and slide
attaching half a floating face
to a poster on a wall?

The first time that a book dissolved
before his eyes was in a French class –
a *trompe-l'oeil* he might have said
had language not already left him
soundless, dropping like a dead thing,
waking later with no answer
for the problem he'd become.

One consultant reassured
his parents it could be controlled;
then turned to tell him how he shared
pathology with Caesar and
perhaps as well with Dostoevsky,
which seemed scarcely consolation
for permanent uncertainty.

Sunlight glancing off the sea
disturbs a shining worm that sleeps
behind his eye. And as it swims
it imitates the filament
within the naked bulb he dreads
which hangs behind a door that opens
only inwards and whose sudden
flashing is the final warning
the handle is about to turn.

FOR MJB WHEREVER THIS MAY FIND HIM

To us he seemed not quite a hero.
We acknowledged he had flaws
but wished as well that we'd the flair
to share his imperfections sometimes.
With beguiling lack of guilt
he'd own up to the frailties
("fainted from my polio jab")
that made his cowardice disarming
contrast to the stiff-lipped style
("I've a floppy lower one")
absorbed from stories of a war
that ended just inside our lifetime.

Boasting of his appetite
for Scotch, he'd loudly speculate
about his liver while we coped
with keeping down a quart of mild;
and let it slip that he enjoyed
occasional (nudge, wink) liaisons
with an older woman, married
maybe or divorced. And when
we sneered at hints of sexual exploits
outside our experience
we never really knew how much
could be written off as fiction.

You could call him in a small way
our prophet of the sixties, who'd
caught a corner of the vision
but scarcely made the most of it.
His manifesto's best expressions
fell well short of revolution:
his trump card was he wasn't Warhol
half a world away – whose point
we missed but might in any case
have reckoned less persuasive than
this not-so-radical example
acted out in Middlesex.

I saw him last a few years older,
lunching in a pub off Fleet Street.
When he returned to work he would be
sacked, he said, for wildly careless
checking of the finance page.
He laughed to launch his unconcern
at editors and readers who
thought figures were significant:
but I was watching the decade
receding wave-like, sucking sand
from soles and toes dug in against
the undertow of desperation.

SNAPSHOT

Abandoned in a drawer for years
she does not blink as I expose her.

She was not smiling when I took the picture
and is not now. Why should she,
knowing what she hadn't seen before:
that we are strangers?
More constant than my memory,
she's accusing me of being someone else.

I can't outstare her
and she won't turn away. With carefulness
that's scarcely true to life
neither can I,
until I choose to own up to her face.

PILLAR BOX

It was always dark
as I remember it
being winter
and late as we could manage.

Without moving we would circle
that obstacle between us
fixed upon the private corner
where our lives had different ways to go.
This was the turning point
to which we kept returning,
eyes meeting as we parted,
seeking without touching
to keep in touch.

Urgently scribbling a conversation
we added postscript after postscript
to keep the correspondence going
until we filled the space available.

Then we said see you
tomorrow or next week
as if it didn't matter.

WARNING OFF

The image of her bright hooped shirt,
silky like a jockey's colours,
is riding rings around my heart.

"He's always had a soft spot for me,"
she confides. "And now I've told him
why it couldn't work." I'm glad,
poor sod, and sorry for him too;
for sitting near her day on day
must make it hard to hide devotion.
She keeps cool and gracious: patient
with his pestering, she'll meet him
sometimes where she feels she can
and smile to tell him when she can't.

"He's hoping I might change my mind."
Again, poor sod: her gentleness
is worked inside her head to something
else on nights like this when weary
words reshape themselves to form
a well-worn, wanted phrase or saying –

just as I know I'll replay
this conversation and convince
myself it really did conceal
no coded messages for me.

FINDING THE WAY

She told me she'd once walked with two small boys
who feared, because she smoked, that she might die.
I said I saw their point. I think we laughed.

The stream was running deeper than we thought
in such a hot, dry summer. But the stones
projected high enough to let us trace
a silly zig-zag, hands clasped in surprise
that we were playing games. And standing on
a slab amid cascades I said, out loud:
No one's ever been just here before.

Beside the fallen mills for dyeing silks
we joked that rocks got permanently tinted
by water that might stain us too. In fact
I knew no shade could linger there but black
for widows' weeds: and this perhaps was why
I took care to see my feet stayed dry
though she, it seemed, was willing to get wet.

DUNGENESS

Descending from the Weald of careful landscapes
we stumbled on a shambles,
a shanty town on shingle,
Soweto-by-the-sea without the sunshine.

We drove, wide-eyed, along the narrow roadway
and wondered in the mist if
we'd conjured the existence
of Toytown with its trainset and its power pack.

Were these magic shabby buildings models
of unfrequented corners
in our personal home counties
thrown up in haste to slack a morning's tension;

a last resort where urban softies find
there's something to be said
for walking near an edge
and leaning into horizontal drizzle?

So setting out, a pair of raw explorers,
we crunched substantial pebbles,
untangled tarry netting
and haggled with the natives for fresh crab.

While Tunbridge may be tidier in winter
we'd care for wilder living,
we pretended, scuttling homeward
to a street that's swept but seldom by the wind.

IN GRANADA

Such delight should not be disembodied
nor her joy confined forever
to just the words that she could scribble
in a pair of bedside journal entries.

What she wrote, amazed at the Alhambra,
tugs my throat while I re-read it –
a jolt the end of every sentence
as I make the effort to continue
past the fear she'll tell me next
of details I've forgotten.

For she won't talk again of falling water.
This paper version of her vision
is what survives to imitate
that eagerness for sharing something new.

We came closer to the Jewish God
in Arab gardens, as like Eden
as any we'd expect to see
prepared by men who let green shade and water
overgrow all evidence
of effort in their building.

Streams were running shallow in the channels,
the fountains arching not so high
before she nudged me to recall
those warm spice smells in Pollinario's,
where Lorca ate his lunch and so did we.

NOTHING OUTWARD

There was unease sulking in the bass line
the whole morning
while we were driving down through Worcestershire,
with reminders from the radio between us
of the issue that was pushing us apart.
Each lyric seemed contrived to make us draw
another inference of infidelity –
a fact which neither of us could admit
sufficiently to reach and turn it off.

Shame whined meanly in the treble clef,
in shrill insistence
that nothing outward had been untoward
and that it hadn't mattered when attraction
was hastily denied and then admitted.
But even if we said a glimpse of glances
had caught the full extent of indiscretion,
could we resolve all tension in the theme
of betrayal lying only with the flesh?

CONVERSATION PIECE

The silence stretched between us
seemed crosswise like a pane of glass
for us to mime through. And the ends
were somewhere else until
it turned on us and placed
the start and finish in our hands.
We wondered, would it snap
if we increased the tension?

At first we held it horizontal,
as if to stretcher wounded feelings;
but then, when drapes we'd spread
for softening sharp edges
kept slipping off, we stood it upright
like an empty placard
or a whitewashed closed-down shopfront
with finger-printed final offers.

SHARP PRACTICE

Out beyond my double-glazing
the early sun is playing on a wall
that's regular as brickwork ought to be;
yet as the light creeps low and probes it,
undercutting structure with sharp shadows,
I must admit it seems to be subsiding.

What is true is weeds have squeezed
as usual through foundations. Other somethings
root between the kerbstones, nibble at
the edges of our rights of way,
where I have noticed magpies getting bolder
alongside wheels which guarantee them carrion.

Short-term enterprise exploits
the narrow gap by making small adjustments
of claw-to-snout and shallow-planted sort.
The furtive opportunist deals
not in mergers or through major coups
but by taking over what is spare.

We may chatter of a rat-race
to justify the kind of greed we're good at
and fancy to be natural. In fact
the smartest of us need to watch
our backs for stealthy claimants, mobile-phoneless,
that pounce when any fellow creature falters.

THE WHISPERING KNIGHTS
(Rollright Stones, Oxfordshire, 1996)

They are conspiring in a turnip field.
Shapes of muffled men are shifting,
seen then unseen, up against the distant
winter-naked trees as stark as stakes.
They lean together, inclining to intrigue,
huddled by the heart-shaped block
they had supported. Its fall portrays at once
the end of trust and crash of their ambition.

The moon-faced roots beneath these stock-still feet
are icons of stupidity;
yet, severed and with features slashed, each one
could occupy a quasi-prophet's post.
Scarecrows, with their twists of bony twigs
that merely look like fire-black hands,
are worthy working cousins to the Guy,
the true mock-man with no use but abuse.

The destiny of plotters turned to stone,
not stoned to pulp, is to be frozen
always in exposure. This attainder
removing every right of hiding place
makes permanent an anguish stretched across
the moment of discovery.
Treason's dream goes nightmare or comes true;
traitors' aims stay crimes unless they're crowned.

GLASTONBURY TOR
(Richard Winter, last Abbot of Glastonbury, executed 1539)

A storm was driving from the east.
Great trees were falling; men of reason
looked for shelter; cowards fled their posts.
And who could turn clenched face towards the riders
coming with the wind behind them?

Then he was carried to a hilltop
overlooking his whole world;
and there one said to him, "All this is mine
to take away from anyone I choose
who will not use it as I wish."

The stones below: had they already
turned themselves to bread for him –
the means of his existence and its meaning?
Perhaps long arches never rise to heaven
quite without ambition's yeast.

On a pinnacle and trapped
between the red hot iron of kings
and God, there was no place for him to stand
but on the wind, believing for a time
an angel or a Pope might catch him.

TO WHOM IT MAY CONCERN

When I heard the way they'd treated you
I wanted, very calmly,
to crush my glass against the table top.

And that would testify
I hadn't anything to do with them –
not the border clerks
who fingered through your papers,
nor the authors of their picklock questions,
shaped to make the wrong replies slide out
like bolts drawn slowly back across a trapdoor.

I wanted to shout down their smug assumption
of my mute agreement
to brand you, steal your clothes and make you dance.

Denials alone won't do
for those who make their own small ugly choices.
I needed, very simply,
to know if God could answer
the question of how far the likes of us
should take an inkling of complicity
when we remember how they treated you.